501
Things to Spot

Layla Temesgen

igloobooks

Ella and Freya are best friends and they love exploring together.

Ella   **Freya**

Can you spot them hiding in each picture in this book?
Once you have found them, there will be other things
to spot in each picture, too. Let's have a practice.

Can you find Ella and Freya at the
play park on the opposite page?

Well done!
Now you've found
Ella and Freya,
see if you can spot
these things, too!

2 slides

4 springy seats

6 sandcastles

Teddy Bears' Picnic

Ella and Freya are having a picnic with
the teddy bears at Rainbow Meadow.
Can you spot them in this picture?

Can you find all of
these other things
at the picnic, too?

2 squirrels

4 green butterflies

5 blue birds

6 lollipops

8 honey drinks

10 cupcakes

berries

crisps

Princess Ball

Ella and Freya are having a wonderful time at the royal palace ball. Can you spot them among all of the guests?

Can you find all of these other items at the ball, too?

1 fruit bowl

2 disco balls

3 purses

4 pink balloons

5 tiaras

10 candles

Mermaids' Lagoon

Ella and Freya are playing with the mermaids in their magical lagoon. Can you spot them amongst the pretty coral?

Can you find all of these other items in the lagoon?

1 mermaid castle

3 dolphins

4 starfish

6 seahorses

7 seashells

10 stripy fish

Pretty Pet Parlor

Ella and Freya have taken their puppies to the Pet Parlor. Can you spot them among all the animals?

Can you find these things at the parlor, too?

2 spotty cushions

3 stripy leads

5 perfume bottles

8 pet brushes

9 soapy sponges

10 paw prints

Candy Land

Ella and Freya have decided to visit Candy Land! There are lots of yummy treats to eat. Can you spot them in this picture?

Can you find all of these items in Candy Land?

1 gingerbread house

3 owls

6 ice lollies

7 giant sweets

8 strawberries

10 candy canes

Beautiful Ballerinas

Ella and Freya love dancing ballet with all of their friends. Can you spot them in this busy ballet class?

Can you find all of these items in this ballet class as well?

3 flower headbands

4 purple tutus

5 pink ribbons

7 hair brushes

9 roses

10 kit bags

Flower Fairies

Ella and Freya are visiting the fairies in Fairyland. Can you spot where they are playing?

Can you find all of these items, too?

2 frogs

3 purple toadstools

5 bags of fairy dust

6 lilies

9 bumblebees

10 dragonflies

Circus Fun

Ella and Freya are having a great time at the circus. Can you spot where they are?

Can you find all of these items in the big top?

1 bicycle

3 cameras

4 pink spotlights

7 binoculars

8 circus flyers

10 juggling balls

WaterWorld

Ella and Freya are having a wonderful time at the water park! Can you spot them among all of their friends?

Can you find all of these items as well?

3 boats

4 pink sunbeds

5 umbrellas

7 rubber rings

8 stripy towels

10 goggles

Street Party

Ella and Freya are having a wonderful party with all of the friends they've made. Can you spot them among the guests?

Can you find all of these items at the party, too?

2 firework wheels

5 speakers

6 slices of cake

8 paper lanterns

10 streamers

20 party bags

Well Done!

You found Ella and Freya in each picture!
How closely were you looking though?
Each of these 10 things appear in every picture as well.

sunflower   wand   dolly   teddy   jewelry box

ladybug   crown   rabbit   mouse   pink satchel

Why don't you
go back to the start
and see
if you can
spot them all!

Bonus!
Hidden somewhere within this book is
Charlie the Crab. Can you find him?